Building a successful online business

Building a Successful Online Business" is an informative guide that provides readers with the essential tools, strategies, and resources needed to start and grow a profitable online business. From identifying your niche and target audience to developing a marketing strategy, creating a unique value proposition, and managing finances, this ebook covers all the key aspects of building a successful online business. With practical tips, real-life examples, and recommended reading materials, this ebook is the ultimate resource for anyone looking to turn their online business dreams into a reality.

I. Introduction

- Definition of online business
- Advantages of starting an online business
- Overview of the ebook's contents

II. Planning and Preparation

- Identifying your business niche and target audience
- Conducting market research and competitor analysis
- Creating a business plan
- Choosing a business name and domain name
- Setting up a website and choosing an e-commerce platform

III. Creating and Marketing Your Product or Service

- Developing a unique value proposition
- Creating a product or service that meets your audience's needs
- Developing a marketing strategy, including social media and email marketing
- Building your brand identity and establishing trust with your audience
- Using SEO to improve your website's visibility

IV. Managing Your Online Business

- Managing your finances and cash flow
- Building a customer service team
- Managing inventory and shipping logistics
- Improving website user experience
- Scaling your business and creating additional revenue streams

V. Conclusions and Tips for Success

- Recap of key points
- Additional tips for success in online business
- Encouragement to take action and start building your online business

VI. Additional Resources

- Recommended tools and resources for building an online business
- Additional reading and learning materials

I. Introduction

Definition of online business

An online business is a type of business that primarily operates over the internet, allowing customers to purchase products or services online through a website or e-commerce platform. An online business may also provide customer support, marketing, and other business functions through digital channels. Online businesses can range from small startups run by a single individual to larger corporations with teams of employees working remotely from various locations. Some examples of online businesses include e-commerce stores, online marketplaces, digital product creators, and software-as-a-service (SaaS) companies.

Advantages of starting an online business

Starting an online business has several advantages over traditional brick-and-mortar businesses, including:

1. Lower startup costs: Starting an online business generally requires less capital investment than starting a physical store or office, as you can operate from anywhere with an internet connection and often do not need to rent a physical space.

2. Greater flexibility: An online business can be run from anywhere and at any time, allowing entrepreneurs to work from home or while traveling. This also provides greater flexibility for employees, who can work remotely from different locations.

3. Wider audience reach: An online business can reach a global audience, allowing businesses to expand their customer base beyond their local area.

4. Lower marketing costs: Online marketing methods, such as social media and email marketing, are often more cost-effective than traditional advertising methods.

5. Easier to track and analyze data: Online businesses have access to a wealth of data, including website traffic, sales data, and customer behavior. This data can be used to make informed business decisions and improve the customer experience.

6. Increased scalability: Online businesses can easily scale up or down depending on demand, without the need for additional physical space or resources.

Overall, starting an online business offers greater flexibility, lower costs, and the potential for greater profits and growth compared to traditional brick-and-mortar businesses.

Overview of the ebook's contents

The ebook, "Building a Successful Online Business," is designed to provide readers with a comprehensive guide to starting and growing a successful online business. The book is divided into several sections, each of which focuses on a different aspect of building an online business.

In the first section, readers will learn about the planning and preparation required to start an online business, including how to identify a niche, conduct market research, create a business plan, choose a business name and domain name, and set up a website and e-commerce platform.

The second section of the book focuses on creating and marketing your product or service. This section covers topics such as developing a unique value proposition, creating a product or service that meets your audience's needs, developing a marketing strategy, building your brand identity, and using SEO to improve your website's visibility.

The third section of the book focuses on managing your online business, including managing your finances and cash flow, building a customer service team, managing inventory and shipping logistics, improving website user experience, and scaling your business and creating additional revenue streams.

Finally, the book concludes with additional tips for success in online business, along with recommended tools and resources for building an online business and additional reading and learning materials.

By the end of the book, readers will have a solid understanding of how to start and grow a successful online business, and will be equipped with the knowledge and tools they need to succeed in the competitive world of e-commerce and digital business.

II. Planning and Preparation

Identifying your business niche and target audience

Identifying your business niche and target audience is a critical first step in building a successful online business. Here are some tips to help you identify your niche and target audience:

1. Identify your passions and expertise: Look for areas where you have knowledge and experience, as this can help you identify a niche that you are passionate about and where you can add value.

2. Conduct market research: Research your potential market and identify gaps in the market that your business could fill. Look at competitors' websites, social media, and other marketing materials to see what they are doing and what you can do differently.

3. Define your ideal customer: Think about the characteristics of your ideal customer, such as age, gender, income level, geographic location, and interests. This will help you tailor your marketing and product development efforts to their needs.

4. Use data to inform your decisions: Use tools like Google Analytics, social media analytics, and customer surveys to gather data about your audience and their preferences. This data can help you make informed decisions about your business strategy and marketing efforts.

5. Refine your niche and target audience over time: As your business grows and evolves, you may need to refine your niche and target audience. Keep an eye on market trends and listen to feedback from your customers to ensure that your business remains relevant and competitive.

By identifying your business niche and target audience, you can create products and services that meet their needs and build a loyal customer base. This is a critical step in building a successful online business that can grow and thrive over time.

Conducting market research and competitor analysis

Conducting market research and competitor analysis is a crucial step in building a successful online business. Here are some tips to help you conduct effective market research and competitor analysis:

1. Define your research goals: Before you begin your research, define your research goals and objectives. This will help you focus your research efforts and ensure that you gather the information you need to make informed decisions.

2. Identify your target market: Identify your target market and their needs, interests, and preferences. Use online tools like Google Trends and social media analytics to gather data about your target market.

3. Analyze your competitors: Identify your competitors and analyze their products, services, marketing strategies, and pricing. Use tools like SEMrush and Ahrefs to analyze their website traffic and search rankings.

4. Conduct customer surveys: Use customer surveys to gather feedback about your product or service and your competitors. This can help you identify areas for improvement and make informed decisions about your business strategy.

5. Stay up-to-date on market trends: Stay up-to-date on market trends and changes in consumer behavior. This can help you identify new opportunities and adjust your business strategy to stay competitive.

By conducting effective market research and competitor analysis, you can gain a better understanding of your target market, identify gaps in the market that your business can fill, and develop a competitive advantage over your competitors. This is a critical step in building a successful online business that can grow and thrive over time.

Creating a business plan

Creating a business plan is an essential step in building a successful online business. Here are some tips to help you create a business plan:

1. Executive summary: Begin your business plan with an executive summary that outlines your business idea, target market, and key goals.

2. Business description: Provide a detailed description of your business, including your mission statement, vision, and values. This should include details about your product or service, your target market, and your competitive advantage.

3. Market analysis: Conduct a thorough analysis of your target market, including their needs, interests, and preferences. This should also include a competitor analysis to identify gaps in the market that your business can fill.

4. Marketing and sales strategy: Describe your marketing and sales strategy, including how you plan to reach your target market, pricing strategies, and sales channels.

5. Operations plan: Describe your operational processes, including how you plan to deliver your product or service, manage inventory, and fulfill orders.

6. Financial plan: Develop a detailed financial plan that includes projected revenue, expenses, and profits. This should also include a cash flow statement and a break-even analysis.

7. Implementation plan: Outline the steps you will take to implement your business plan, including timelines and milestones.

8. Review and revise: Review and revise your business plan regularly to ensure that it remains relevant and up-to-date.

By creating a thorough and well-structured business plan, you can ensure that you have a solid foundation for your online business. This will help you make informed decisions, secure funding, and set yourself up for long-term success.

Choosing a business name and domain name

Choosing a business name and domain name is an important step in building a successful online business. Here are some tips to help you choose the right name:

1. Make it memorable: Choose a name that is easy to remember and catchy. This will help your business stand out and make it easier for customers to find you online.

2. Make it relevant: Choose a name that is relevant to your business and conveys what you offer. This will help customers understand what you do and what you can offer them.

3. Check for availability: Before you settle on a name, check to see if it is available as a domain name and social media handles. This will ensure that you can use the name consistently across all platforms.

4. Avoid trademark infringement: Avoid using a name that is already trademarked or too similar to an existing business. This can lead to legal issues down the line.

5. Consider SEO: Choose a name that is SEO-friendly and includes relevant keywords. This will make it easier for customers to find your website through search engines.

6. Get feedback: Get feedback from friends, family, and potential customers on your chosen name. This can help you gauge whether the name resonates with your target audience.

By choosing a memorable, relevant, and SEO-friendly business name and domain name, you can help your online business stand out and make it easier for customers to find you.

Setting up a website and choosing an e-commerce platform

Setting up a website and choosing an e-commerce platform are crucial steps in building a successful online business. Here are some tips to help you get started:

1. Choose a website builder: Choose a website builder that suits your needs and skill level. Popular options include WordPress, Wix, and Squarespace.

2. Design your website: Design a website that is user-friendly, visually appealing, and easy to navigate. Make sure your website reflects your brand and showcases your products or services.

3. Add e-commerce functionality: Choose an e-commerce platform that integrates with your website builder. Popular options include Shopify, WooCommerce, and BigCommerce.

4. Set up payment and shipping options: Choose a payment gateway that is secure and easy to use. Set up shipping options that are affordable and reliable.

5. Optimize for SEO: Optimize your website for search engines by including relevant keywords in your content, meta descriptions, and title tags.

6. Test and optimize: Test your website and e-commerce platform to ensure that everything is working smoothly. Make tweaks and optimizations as necessary.

By setting up a website and choosing an e-commerce platform that is user-friendly, secure, and optimized for SEO, you can create a seamless online shopping experience for your customers. This will help you build trust, increase sales, and grow your online business over time.

III. Creating and Marketing Your Product or Service

Developing a unique value proposition

Developing a unique value proposition (UVP) is an important step in building a successful online business. Your UVP is a statement that communicates the unique benefit that your product or service provides to customers. Here are some tips to help you develop a compelling UVP:

1. Identify your target audience: Start by identifying your target audience and their needs, interests, and pain points. This will help you tailor your UVP to their specific needs.

2. Identify your unique selling proposition: Identify what sets your product or service apart from your competitors. This could be a unique feature, a lower price point, better quality, or faster delivery.

3. Focus on benefits, not features: Instead of focusing on the features of your product or service, focus on the benefits that customers will receive. For example, instead of saying "Our software has a user-friendly interface," say "Our software saves you time and frustration by being easy to use."

4. Keep it concise: Your UVP should be concise and easy to understand. Aim for a sentence or two that clearly communicates your unique benefit.

5. Test and refine: Test your UVP with your target audience to see how they respond. Refine your UVP as necessary based on their feedback.

By developing a compelling UVP, you can differentiate yourself from your competitors and communicate the unique value that your product or service provides to customers. This can help you attract and retain customers over time.

Creating a product or service that meets your audience's needs

Creating a product or service that meets your audience's needs is crucial to building a successful online business. Here are some tips to help you create a product or service that resonates with your target audience:

1. Conduct market research: Conduct market research to understand your target audience's needs, preferences, and pain points. Use this information to create a product or service that solves their problems and meets their needs.

2. Create a minimum viable product (MVP): Create a minimum viable product (MVP) that allows you to test your product or service with your target audience. This will help you get feedback and refine your offering before investing too much time and money.

3. Iterate based on feedback: Use feedback from your target audience to iterate and improve your product or service. This will help you create a solution that truly meets their needs and stands out in the market.

4. Focus on quality: Focus on creating a high-quality product or service that exceeds your target audience's expectations. This will help you build trust, establish your brand, and generate positive word-of-mouth.

5. Offer excellent customer service: Offer excellent customer service to ensure that your target audience feels heard and valued. This will help you build loyalty and generate repeat business over time.

By creating a product or service that meets your target audience's needs and exceeds their expectations, you can build a loyal customer base and establish your brand as a trusted solution in the market.

Developing a marketing strategy, including social media and email marketing

Developing a marketing strategy is essential to promoting your online business and attracting customers. Here are some tips to help you develop an effective marketing strategy, including social media and email marketing:

1. Define your target audience: Define your target audience based on their demographics, interests, and behavior. This will help you tailor your marketing messages to their specific needs and preferences.

2. Set marketing goals: Set clear and measurable marketing goals, such as increasing website traffic, generating leads, or increasing sales. This will help you focus your efforts and track your progress over time.

3. Create a content marketing plan: Create a content marketing plan that includes blog posts, videos, social media updates, and other types of content that provide value to your target audience. This will help you attract and engage potential customers.

4. Use social media: Use social media platforms like Facebook, Twitter, and Instagram to promote your business, engage with your target audience, and build your brand. Post regularly and use hashtags to reach new audiences.

5. Use email marketing: Use email marketing to stay in touch with your target audience, promote your products or services, and build relationships over time. Offer exclusive discounts and promotions to encourage sign-ups and engagement.

6. Measure and optimize: Measure your marketing results and optimize your strategy based on what works and what doesn't. Use analytics tools to track website traffic, social media engagement, email open rates, and other key metrics.

By developing a marketing strategy that includes social media and email marketing, you can attract and engage potential customers, build your brand, and generate more leads and sales over time.

Building your brand identity and establishing trust with your audience

Building your brand identity and establishing trust with your audience is key to the success of your online business. Here are some tips to help you build a strong brand and establish trust with your target audience:

1. Define your brand: Define your brand by identifying your unique value proposition, mission, and values. This will help you create a consistent brand identity across all your marketing materials and messaging.

2. Create a strong visual identity: Create a strong visual identity by developing a logo, color scheme, and design elements that reflect your brand personality and values. Use these elements consistently across your website, social media, and other marketing channels.

3. Provide high-quality content: Provide high-quality content that provides value to your target audience. This will help you establish yourself as an expert in your industry and build trust with your audience.

4. Engage with your audience: Engage with your audience by responding to comments and messages on social media, hosting live events and webinars, and soliciting feedback and input. This will help you build relationships and establish trust with your target audience.

5. Provide excellent customer service: Provide excellent customer service by responding promptly to inquiries, addressing customer concerns, and resolving issues quickly and professionally. This will help you build a loyal customer base and generate positive word-of-mouth.

6. Solicit and showcase customer reviews and testimonials: Solicit and showcase customer reviews and testimonials on your website and social media channels. This will help you build credibility and establish trust with potential customers.

By building a strong brand identity and establishing trust with your audience, you can differentiate yourself from competitors, build a loyal customer base, and drive long-term success for your online business.

Using SEO to improve your website's visibility

Search engine optimization (SEO) is the process of optimizing your website to improve its visibility on search engines like Google. Here are some tips to help you use SEO to improve your website's visibility:

1. Conduct keyword research: Conduct keyword research to identify the keywords and phrases your target audience is searching for. Use these keywords strategically in your website content and metadata.

2. Optimize your website structure: Optimize your website structure by creating a clear hierarchy of pages, using descriptive URLs, and optimizing your website speed and mobile responsiveness.

3. Create high-quality content: Create high-quality content that provides value to your target audience. Use keywords strategically, but don't keyword stuff, as this can hurt your search engine rankings.

4. Build high-quality backlinks: Build high-quality backlinks by creating content that other websites want to link to and by reaching out to relevant websites to request backlinks.

5. Optimize your metadata: Optimize your website metadata, including page titles, descriptions, and header tags, to include keywords and provide clear, concise information about your website content.

6. Use local SEO tactics: If you have a local business, use local SEO tactics, such as including your location in your content and metadata, optimizing your Google My Business profile, and earning reviews from local customers.

By using SEO to improve your website's visibility, you can attract more organic traffic from search engines, increase your website's authority and credibility, and ultimately generate more leads and sales for your online business.

IV. Managing Your Online Business

Managing your finances and cash flow

Managing your finances and cash flow is essential for the success of your online business. Here are some tips to help you manage your finances effectively:

1. Set up a separate business bank account: Setting up a separate business bank account will help you keep your personal and business finances separate, making it easier to track your income and expenses.

2. Keep track of your income and expenses: Keep detailed records of your income and expenses, including invoices, receipts, and bank statements. This will help you track your cash flow and identify areas where you can reduce expenses or increase revenue.

3. Create a budget: Create a budget that outlines your projected income and expenses for the year. This will help you plan for expenses and ensure that you have enough cash flow to cover your costs.

4. Use accounting software: Use accounting software like QuickBooks or Xero to manage your finances and automate tasks like invoicing and expense tracking.

5. Invoice promptly and follow up on overdue payments: Invoice your customers promptly and follow up on overdue payments to ensure that you have a steady cash flow.

6. Manage your inventory: If you sell physical products, manage your inventory carefully to avoid overstocking or understocking. This will help you avoid cash flow problems and ensure that you have the products you need to fulfill customer orders.

By managing your finances and cash flow effectively, you can ensure the long-term success of your online business.

Building a customer service team

Building a customer service team is essential for providing excellent support to your customers and ensuring their satisfaction with your products or services. Here are some tips to help you build an effective customer service team:

1. Define your customer service goals: Define your customer service goals and create a plan to achieve them. This will help you identify the skills and experience you need in your customer service team.

2. Hire the right people: Hire people who have the skills and experience you need to provide excellent customer service. Look for people who are empathetic, patient, and have excellent communication skills.

3. Provide training: Provide training to your customer service team to ensure they have the knowledge and skills they need to support your customers. This includes product training, communication skills, and problem-solving skills.

4. Establish clear processes: Establish clear processes for handling customer inquiries, complaints, and returns. This will help your team provide consistent and efficient support to your customers.

5. Use customer service software: Use customer service software like Zendesk or Freshdesk to manage customer inquiries and support tickets. This will help you track customer interactions and ensure that your team is responding to inquiries in a timely manner.

6. Monitor customer feedback: Monitor customer feedback to identify areas where you can improve your customer service. Use customer feedback to make changes to your products or services and improve your customer service processes.

By building a customer service team, you can provide excellent support to your customers and ensure their satisfaction with your products or services. This can help you build a loyal customer base and improve the reputation of your online business.

Managing inventory and shipping logistics

Managing inventory and shipping logistics is an important part of running an online business. Here are some tips to help you manage your inventory and shipping processes effectively:

1. Use inventory management software: Use inventory management software like TradeGecko or Skubana to track your inventory levels and manage stock across multiple sales channels.

2. Set up a system for receiving and processing orders: Set up a system for receiving and processing orders, including packaging and shipping. This can include using a shipping software like ShipStation or ShipBob to automate the process.

3. Choose a reliable shipping carrier: Choose a reliable shipping carrier that offers competitive rates and tracking options. Popular carriers for online businesses include USPS, UPS, and FedEx.

4. Calculate shipping costs: Calculate shipping costs based on the weight and size of your products, as well as the destination. Consider offering free shipping for orders over a certain amount to incentivize customers to purchase more.

5. Use shipping supplies efficiently: Use shipping supplies efficiently to reduce waste and save money. Consider using biodegradable or recycled packaging materials to reduce your environmental impact.

6. Monitor inventory levels and reorder as needed: Monitor your inventory levels and reorder products as needed to avoid stockouts and delays in shipping. Use inventory forecasting tools to help you predict future demand and plan accordingly.

By managing your inventory and shipping logistics effectively, you can ensure that your customers receive their orders on time and with minimal issues. This can help you build a positive reputation and increase customer loyalty.

Improving website user experience

Improving website user experience is essential for keeping visitors engaged and increasing conversions. Here are some tips to help you improve your website user experience:

1. Optimize your website speed: Ensure that your website loads quickly to prevent visitors from leaving due to slow load times. Use website speed testing tools like Google PageSpeed Insights to identify areas for improvement.

2. Simplify your website design: Simplify your website design to make it easier for visitors to navigate and find the information they need. Use clear headings, easy-to-read fonts, and plenty of white space to make your website visually appealing and easy to use.

3. Make your website mobile-friendly: Ensure that your website is mobile-friendly to accommodate the growing number of mobile users. Use responsive design to ensure that your website looks good on all devices.

4. Use clear calls-to-action (CTAs): Use clear and prominent CTAs to guide visitors to take the desired action, such as making a purchase or signing up for a newsletter.

5. Provide helpful content: Provide helpful and informative content that addresses the needs and interests of your target audience. This can include blog posts, how-to guides, and product reviews.

6. Implement user-friendly search functionality: Implement user-friendly search functionality to help visitors find the information or products they are looking for quickly and easily.

By improving your website user experience, you can increase engagement and conversions, and ultimately grow your online business. Remember to regularly test and analyze your website to identify areas for improvement and optimize your website accordingly.

Scaling your business and creating additional revenue streams

Scaling your business and creating additional revenue streams is an important step in growing your online business. Here are some tips to help you scale your business and create additional revenue streams:

1. Expand your product or service offerings: Consider expanding your product or service offerings to meet the needs and interests of your target audience. Conduct market research to identify new opportunities for growth and expansion.

2. Launch a subscription service: Launch a subscription service to provide a steady stream of recurring revenue. This can include offering a monthly subscription box or access to exclusive content or services.

3. Develop partnerships and collaborations: Develop partnerships and collaborations with other businesses or influencers to expand your reach and customer base. This can include co-creating products or services or collaborating on marketing initiatives.

4. Offer consulting or coaching services: If you have expertise in your industry, consider offering consulting or coaching services to help other businesses or individuals achieve their goals.

5. Expand your online presence: Expand your online presence by leveraging social media platforms, launching a YouTube channel, or creating a podcast. This can help you reach new audiences and build your brand.

6. Consider franchising or licensing: If you have a successful business model, consider franchising or licensing it to other entrepreneurs. This can provide a new revenue stream and help you expand your business without taking on all the risk and expenses yourself.

By scaling your business and creating additional revenue streams, you can achieve long-term growth and success. Remember to stay focused on your core values and mission while exploring new opportunities for expansion.

V. Conclusions and Tips for Success

Recap of key points

To recap the key points covered in this ebook on building a successful online business, we discussed the following:

1. Definition and advantages of starting an online business.

2. Identifying your business niche and target audience.

3. Conducting market research and competitor analysis.

4. Creating a business plan.

5. Choosing a business name and domain name.

6. Setting up a website and choosing an e-commerce platform.

7. Developing a unique value proposition.

8. Creating a product or service that meets your audience's needs.

9. Developing a marketing strategy, including social media and email marketing.

10. Building your brand identity and establishing trust with your audience.

11. Using SEO to improve your website's visibility.

12. Managing your finances and cash flow.

13. Building a customer service team.

14. Managing inventory and shipping logistics.

15. Improving website user experience.

16. Scaling your business and creating additional revenue streams.

By implementing these key points, you can build a strong foundation for your online business and achieve long-term success. Remember to regularly analyze and optimize your strategies to stay ahead of the competition and keep your business growing.

Additional tips for success in online business

Here are some additional tips for success in online business:

1. Focus on building a loyal customer base: Building a loyal customer base is critical to the success of any online business. By providing exceptional customer service, delivering quality products or services, and building trust with your audience, you can establish a loyal customer base that will support your business over the long term.

2. Stay up-to-date with technology and trends: Technology and trends in online business are constantly evolving. Staying up-to-date with the latest advancements in technology and trends can help you stay competitive and relevant in your industry.

3. Continuously improve your website and user experience: Your website is the face of your online business. Continuously improving your website and user experience can help you attract and retain customers, improve search engine rankings, and drive sales.

4. Network and collaborate with other entrepreneurs: Networking and collaborating with other entrepreneurs can help you expand your reach, learn from others in your industry, and identify new opportunities for growth and expansion.

5. Stay disciplined and focused: Building a successful online business requires discipline and focus. Create a schedule, set goals, and prioritize your tasks to stay on track and make progress towards your goals.

By following these additional tips, you can further increase your chances of success in your online business. Remember to stay agile, adapt to changes, and continuously work towards improving your business.

Encouragement to take action and start building your online business

Now that you have learned the key points and additional tips for building a successful online business, it's time to take action and start building your own online business. Starting an online business can be a daunting task, but with the right mindset and guidance, it is entirely achievable.

Remember, every successful online business started with an idea and a decision to take action. With the right approach, dedication, and persistence, you can turn your idea into a profitable business that can change your life.

It's time to put your plan into action and take the first steps towards building your online business. Whether it's conducting market research, choosing a business name, or setting up a website, take action today, and move closer to your goals.

So, what are you waiting for? Start building your online business today and turn your dreams into reality!

VI. Additional Resources

Recommended tools and resources for building an online business

Here are some recommended tools and resources for building an online business:

1. Website Builders: Website builders like Wix, Squarespace, and WordPress make it easy to create a professional-looking website without any coding skills.

2. E-commerce Platforms: E-commerce platforms like Shopify, BigCommerce, and WooCommerce provide everything you need to set up and manage an online store, including payment processing, inventory management, and shipping logistics.

3. Email Marketing Software: Email marketing software like Mailchimp, ConvertKit, and Constant Contact help you build and manage email lists, design and send email campaigns, and track engagement metrics.

4. Social Media Management Tools: Social media management tools like Hootsuite, Buffer, and Sprout Social allow you to manage and schedule social media content, track engagement, and analyze performance metrics.

5. Market Research Tools: Market research tools like SurveyMonkey, Google Trends, and SEMrush provide valuable insights into market trends, customer behavior, and competition.

6. Business Planning Software: Business planning software like LivePlan, Enloop, and StratPad help you create professional business plans, financial projections, and investor presentations.

7. Online Courses and Communities: Online courses and communities like Udemy, Coursera, and Reddit offer valuable resources, training, and networking opportunities for entrepreneurs.

By using these tools and resources, you can streamline your operations, improve your marketing efforts, and gain a competitive edge in your industry. Remember to choose the tools that align with your business goals, budget, and needs.

Additional reading and learning materials

Here are some additional reading and learning materials that can help you deepen your knowledge and skills in building an online business:

1. "The Lean Startup" by Eric Ries: This book provides a framework for developing a startup with a focus on building products that customers want.

2. "Jab, Jab, Jab, Right Hook" by Gary Vaynerchuk: This book offers practical advice on social media marketing, including creating engaging content, building a following, and converting followers into customers.

3. "Influence: The Psychology of Persuasion" by Robert Cialdini: This book explores the science of persuasion and provides insights into how to influence customers and stakeholders.

4. "The 4-Hour Work Week" by Timothy Ferriss: This book offers a blueprint for designing a lifestyle business that allows you to work less and live more.

5. "Crush It!: Why Now Is the Time to Cash in on Your Passion" by Gary Vaynerchuk: This book provides a roadmap for turning your passion into a profitable online business.

6. Hubspot Academy: Hubspot offers a wide range of free online courses on marketing, sales, and customer service.

7. Google Analytics Academy: Google offers free online courses on how to use Google Analytics to track and analyze website traffic and user behavior.

8. Coursera: Coursera offers online courses from top universities and industry experts on a variety of business topics, including entrepreneurship, marketing, and e-commerce.

By reading and learning from these materials, you can stay up-to-date on the latest trends and best practices in building a successful online business.

Some helpful Links to Tools

- **Money Robot (Best Backlink Builder Tool)**
- **SEOMedia24 WebP Image Converter Pro**

- **SEOMedia24 Speed up WP and Woo Caching Minification**
- **High quality Backlink Service**
- **High quality Traffic Booster**

Impressum

SEO MEDIA AGENTUR

Eichendorffstr 2a

57518 Betzdorf

Deutschland

Telefon: +49274168989530

Mail: support@seomedia24.com

Verantwortlich gemäß § 18 MStV:

SEO MEDIA AGENTUR

Eichendorffstr 2a

57518 Betzdorf